cooking with
lemons&limes

cooking with
lemons&limes

Brian Glover   *photography by Richard Jung*

RYLAND
PETERS
& SMALL

LONDON NEW YORK

First published in the USA in 2006
by Ryland Peters & Small, Inc.
519 Broadway, 5th Floor
New York, NY 10012

www.rylandpeters.com

10 9 8 7 6 5 4 3 2 1

Library of Congress Cataloging-in-
Publication Data

Glover, Brian, 1958-
  Cooking with lemons & limes /
Brian Glover ; photography by
Richard Jung.
     p. cm.
  Includes index.
  ISBN-13: 978-1-84597-140-3
  ISBN-10: 1-84597-140-X
  1. Cookery (Lemons) 2. Cookery
(Limes) 3. Cookery, International. I.
Title: Cooking with lemons and
limes. II. Title.

TX813.L4G66 2006
641.6'4334--dc22

2005026983

Printed in China

Author's acknowledgements

I'd like to thank my editors at RPS,
Elsa Petersen-Schepelern and
Rachel Lawrence, and Richard Jung
and Linda Tubby for making the food
look so good.

Senior Designer Steve Painter
Commissioning Editor
    Elsa Petersen-Schepelern
Editor Rachel Lawrence
Production Gemma Moules
Art Director Anne-Marie Bulat
Editorial Director Julia Charles

Food Stylist Linda Tubby
Prop Stylist Róisîn Nield
Indexer Penelope Kent

Notes

• When using the zest of lemons or
limes in a dish, try to find organic or
unwaxed fruits and wash well. If you
can only find treated fruit, scrub well
in warm soapy water and rinse.

• Lemons and limes will yield up
more juice when warm. Cover them
in hot water in a bowl and leave for
5–10 minutes. Pressing them down
hard on a work surface will also help
to release the juice.

• All spoon measurements are level,
unless otherwise specified.

• Ovens should be preheated to the
specified temperature. Recipes in
this book were tested using a regular
oven. If using a fan-assisted oven,
follow the manufacturer's instructions
for adjusting temperatures.

• All eggs are medium, unless
otherwise specified. Recipes
containing raw or partially cooked
egg, or raw fish or shellfish, should
not be served to the very young or
old, any one with a compromised
immune system or pregnant women.

• Sterilize preserving jars before use.
Wash in hot, soapy water and rinse
in boiling water. Place in a large
saucepan and cover with hot water.
Bring to the boil, covered, and boil
for 15 minutes. Turn off the heat and
leave the jars in the hot water until
just before they are to be filled, then
invert onto clean paper towels to dry.
Sterilize the lids for 5 minutes, by
boiling or following manufacturer's
instructions. Jars should be filled and
sealed while they are still hot.

contents

lemons and limes: kitchen essentials

When cooking I reach for lemons almost as often as salt, black pepper, and olive oil. A squeeze of lemon can make a lackluster dish sing, and with good olive oil and seasoning, lemon juice makes the best dressing for a crisp salad or for a piece of grilled fish. Lemon's tartness pierces through rich food and brings out flavor in a subtler, more complex way than salt—certainly, it's a healthier option.

Lemons originated in Asia, but the Mediterranean is their spiritual home. Lemons grown on the Amalfi coast or in Sicily are still the most prized and the well-nigh holy trinity of olive oil, garlic, and lemon instantly conjures up the smell and taste of Mediterranean food. As well as growing lemons, the Italians are past masters at using them—whether scattering a gremolata of garlic and lemon over a hearty stew, pressing lemons and olives together to make a superb citrus-scented oil, or using lemons to flavor delicious gelati or drinks, such as Limoncello. But all round the Mediterranean, in North Africa, Greece, and the Middle East, people use lemons almost every time they cook—in fruit and vegetable dishes, on meat, chicken, or fish, and to flavor a host of sweet puddings, cakes, and cookies.

Lemon trees won't thrive where the climate is too hot, but thankfully limes do. Smaller, sharper, but more intensely fragrant than lemons, limes work with exotic, spicy flavors. Recipes from Southeast Asia, Africa, South America, Mexico, and the Caribbean use limes freely with herbs and spices such as cilantro, ginger, galangal, chile, cardamom, and cumin. Lime juice is used to "cook" fish, to pickle meat, and to act as a sharp antidote to chiles' heat. In Western-style cooking, you can often experiment by using limes instead of lemons: the warm, almost gingery flavor of lime is exquisite in ice creams, custards, sweet tarts, and buttery cakes.

Yes, lemons and limes are essentials in the kitchen; use them both depending on your mood. Sometimes I want the sharp clarity of lemon, sometimes the richer fragrance of lime; the thing I'd hate is to be without either.

SOUPS AND SALADS

1 lb. large uncooked shrimp

1 tablespoon sunflower or peanut oil

1 teaspoon grated lime zest

5½ cups fish or chicken stock

2 lemon grass stalks, thinly sliced

3 garlic cloves, halved

1 inch piece of fresh ginger, unpeeled and sliced

a small bunch of fresh cilantro, chopped, stalks reserved

3 fresh or dried kaffir lime leaves*

a bunch of spring onions, thinly sliced, green and white parts separated

2–3 small hot red chiles, halved and seeded

1 large carrot, cut into matchstick strips

2–3 tablespoons Thai fish sauce

freshly squeezed juice of up to 2 limes

1–2 pinches of caster sugar

6 oz. Asian greens, such as bok choy or mustard greens, sliced

sea salt and freshly ground black pepper

lime wedges, to serve

a ridged stovetop grill pan or skillet

SERVES 4

It's the lime juice and kaffir lime leaves that make this hot and sour soup so addictively delicious. The lime cuts through the heat of the chile peppers and counterbalances the salty piquancy of the other essential ingredient—Thai fish sauce or nam pla. While shrimp work particularly well here, you could also use strips of flash-fried squid or strips of white fish.

hot and sour soup

with shrimp

Shell and devein the shrimp, then toss 8–12 of them in the oil and lime zest and season with a little salt. Roughly chop the remainder into 3–4 pieces each. Keep all the shrimp chilled while you make the soup.

Put the stock, lemon grass, garlic, ginger, cilantro stalks, kaffir lime leaves, the green parts of the onions, and 1–2 chiles in a saucepan, bring to the boil and simmer, covered, for 15–20 minutes. Strain and return to the pan.

Add the carrot and cook for 3–4 minutes, then add the white part of the onion and the chopped shrimp. Simmer for a few minutes, then add fish sauce and lime juice to taste. Adjust the seasoning with salt, pepper, and a pinch or two of sugar. The soup should be fairly piquant and sharp.

Meanwhile, heat a ridged stovetop grill pan or skillet until hot, add the reserved whole shrimp and quickly fry them for 2–3 minutes until they turn pink and opaque.

Reheat the soup if necessary and stir in the Asian greens and most of the cilantro leaves, then ladle the hot soup into bowls and add 2–3 whole shrimp to each bowl. Garnish with the remaining cilantro leaves and remaining chile, shredded, then serve with lime wedges.

*Note Kaffir lime leaves come from a southeast Asian variety of lime. The rough peel and the leaves are exceedingly fragrant. Fresh leaves are sometimes available in Asian stores and they freeze well. Dried ones in jars are available in most large supermarkets.

This recipe is based on a classic southern Italian way of cooking zucchini. It makes a lovely first course, either alone or as part of a mixed antipasti, accompanied by some grilled bell peppers, bottled artichokes, or a roasted eggplant dip. Alternatively, try it with a simply broiled or grilled lamb steak.

1½–1¾ lb. small zucchini

¼ teaspoon dried red pepper flakes

1 tablespoon extra virgin olive oil

6 oz. feta cheese, sliced and crumbled into fairly large pieces

¼ cup toasted pine nuts

sea salt and freshly ground black pepper

LEMON, CAPER, AND MINT DRESSING

¼ cup extra virgin olive oil

1 tablespoon freshly squeezed lemon juice

½ teaspoon balsamic vinegar, plus extra to taste

½ teaspoon grated lemon zest

1–2 garlic cloves, finely chopped

1 tablespoon chopped fresh mint, plus a few whole leaves to garnish

2 tablespoons chopped fresh flat-leaf parsley

2 tablespoons small salted capers, rinsed and soaked in cold water for 10 minutes, then drained

a ridged stovetop grill pan

a baking sheet (optional)

SERVES 4–6

grilled zucchini and feta salad

with lemon, caper, and mint dressing

Cut the zucchini lengthways into 2-inch slices. Put in a colander and toss with 1 teaspoon salt. Leave for 30–60 minutes to drain in the sink, then rinse and dry on paper towels.

Season with lots of pepper and the pepper flakes, if using. Add the oil and toss to coat. Heat a ridged stovetop grill pan until hot and grill the zucchini for 6–8 minutes, turning once, until well browned and just tender. Alternatively, heat a broiler to hot, put the zucchini on a baking sheet, and broil for 6–8 minutes, turning once. Put the zucchini in a dish.

To make the dressing, put the oil, lemon juice, balsamic vinegar, lemon zest, garlic, and chopped mint and parsley in a bowl and whisk well. Stir in the capers and pour the dressing over the zucchini. Cover and set aside for 30–60 minutes for the flavors to marry. Just before serving, mix in the feta cheese and serve sprinkled with the pine nuts and a few mint leaves.

1½ lb. cleaned small squid

1 tablespoon peanut oil

a pinch of dried red pepper flakes

a handful of peppery salad leaves,
such as mizuna, baby red
mustard or arugula

2 large carrots, cut into
matchstick strips

4 oz. snow peas, finely shredded

1 small red onion, halved and very
thinly sliced

sea salt and freshly
ground black pepper

LIME, CHILE, AND GARLIC
DRESSING

2 garlic cloves

1 small red chile,
seeded and thinly sliced

1–2 teaspoons light brown sugar

3–4 tablespoons freshly
squeezed lime juice

1–2 tablespoons Thai fish sauce

TO SERVE

4 shallots, thinly sliced

vegetable oil, for shallow-frying

leaves from a small bunch
of fresh cilantro

a few fresh mint or Thai basil
leaves, torn

1 mild red chile, thinly
sliced (optional)

*a ridged stovetop grill pan or
nonstick skillet*

SERVES 4

*It's the dressing that is the star of the show here—garlicky
and at once sour with lime, sweet with brown sugar, and
salty with the deeply savory flavor of Thai fish sauce.
You can use this dressing on all kinds of ingredients—on
shredded cold chicken or pork, or on strips of hot, seared
steak, for instance.*

squid salad

with lime, chile, and garlic dressing

To prepare the squid, cut off the tentacles in one piece. Open the
body to make a rough rectangle and score it lightly with a cross-hatch
of cuts. Toss the squid with the oil, pepper flakes, and a little salt.
Cover and leave to marinate in the refrigerator.

Meanwhile, to make the dressing, crush the garlic with a pinch of
salt in a mortar and pestle, then work in the chile, pounding it lightly.
Gradually work in 1 teaspoon sugar, 3 tablespoons lime juice, and
1 tablespoon fish sauce, then let stand for 10 minutes. Add more
sugar, lime juice or fish sauce, to taste.

Put the shallots in a sieve. Sprinkle with 1 teaspoon salt, leave for
30 minutes, drain in the sink, then rinse and dry on paper towels.
Heat a shallow layer of oil in a small skillet over medium heat and
cook the shallots gently until golden brown and crisp. Drain on
paper towels.

Heat a ridged stovetop grill pan or nonstick skillet until very hot. Add
the squid, in batches if necessary, and sear very quickly for 1 minute
on each side. The squid will curl and turn opaque and brown in
places. Arrange the salad leaves on plates or a serving platter and
sprinkle with half the cilantro leaves. Toss the vegetables with about
2 tablespoons of the dressing, then arrange on the salad leaves. Add
the squid, then finish the salad with the remaining cilantro, the mint
leaves, the crisp-fried shallots, and chile, if using. Finally, sprinkle with
the remaining dressing and serve immediately.

Ceviche (sometimes spelled seviche) is a South American dish of fish marinated in lime juice. The acid in the lime juice turns the fish opaque and changes its texture, making it seem cooked. It goes without saying that you should use the very freshest fish available—sole, snapper, tilapia, and seabass are all good. Serve with plenty of crusty bread to soak up the dressing.

ceviche

with red onion, avocado, and lime

1½ lb. very fresh skinless white fish fillets

1 red onion, halved and thinly sliced

1 hot red or green chile, seeded and finely chopped

1 teaspoon grated fresh ginger

freshly squeezed juice of 6 limes

½–1 teaspoon sugar, plus extra to taste

½ teaspoon coriander seeds, toasted and ground

5 tablespoons mild olive oil

finely grated zest of 1 small lime

2 ripe avocados, peeled, pitted, and sliced

1 ripe but firm papaya, peeled, seeded, and sliced

10 oz. cooked peeled shrimp

a small bunch of fresh cilantro

sea salt and freshly ground black pepper

salad leaves, to serve (optional)

SERVES 6 AS A STARTER

Cut the fish into strips or chunks. Sprinkle half the onion in a glass dish and put the fish on top, sprinkling half the chopped chile and the ginger over the top. Pour in the juice of 5 of the limes, cover and leave to marinate in the refrigerator for 1–1½ hours, spooning the juice over the fish once or twice.

Meanwhile, put the remaining onion in a sieve and pour over a kettle of boiling water. Drain thoroughly, then put in a non-metallic bowl and toss with 1 tablespoon of the remaining lime juice, ½ teaspoon sugar and the ground coriander seeds. Cover and let stand for 20–30 minutes, tossing once or twice.

Put the oil in a small bowl and whisk in the liquid from the onions. Add salt and pepper to taste, then whisk in the lime zest. Adjust the flavor with extra lime juice or sugar to taste. Drain the liquid from the fish and discard the onion, ginger, and chile. In a large glass bowl, toss the fish, marinated onion, avocado, papaya, shrimp, and dressing. Finely chop half the fresh cilantro and mix into the ceviche.

Put a pile of salad leaves, if using, on each plate and spoon over the ceviche, sprinkle with the remaining cilantro leaves and the remaining chile, then serve.

½ cup wild rice

½ cup brown basmati rice

½ cup white long-grain rice

½ cup currants, soaked in warm water for 10 minutes, then drained

⅓ cup dried cherries, chopped if large

1 large bulb of fennel, trimmed and chopped, feathery tops reserved

1 teaspoon crushed cumin seeds

a bunch of scallions, sliced

⅓ cup blanched split almonds, toasted

⅓ cup shelled and blanched pistachio nuts, chopped

3 tablespoons chopped fresh cilantro

freshly ground black pepper

cos lettuce leaves, to serve

PRESERVED LEMON DRESSING

5 tablespoons extra virgin olive oil

1–2 tablespoons freshly squeezed lemon juice

1 garlic clove, crushed

2 tablespoons chopped Preserved Lemons (page 61)

1–2 pinches of sugar

SERVES 6–8

If you have a phobic reaction to rice salad from sampling one too many of the bland mass caterers variety, this one may well bring you back into the fold. The essential ingredient is preserved lemons, which you can find in Middle Eastern stores or large supermarkets, or see page 61 to make your own. If you make the ones in olive oil, you can add a little of the oil to the dressing to add even more of their lovely mellow yet sharp flavor. This is good with many things, such as fish, chicken, cold roast pork, or lamb.

rice salad

with preserved lemon dressing

Cook each variety of rice in a separate saucepan of boiling water over medium heat until tender. The wild rice takes up to 40 minutes*, brown rice about 25 minutes, and long-grain rice should be tender in 15 minutes. Drain the rice into a colander. Rinse briefly with hot water, then leave to drain well, fluffing up with a fork after 5 minutes.

Meanwhile, make the dressing. Put the oil and the lemon juice in a bowl, whisk well, then whisk in the garlic and preserved lemon. Season to taste with pepper and sugar. Toss the cooked rice with half the dressing, the currants, and the cherries.

Heat the remaining oil in a skillet and cook the fennel and crushed cumin seeds gently for 5 minutes until softened but not browned. Add the scallions and cook for another 1–2 minutes. Stir into the rice with the nuts and coriander and fennel tops, chopped. Let the salad stand for 30 minutes, then stir in the remaining dressing and serve with the lettuce leaves.

Note To cut down the cooking time for wild rice, soak it for 30 minutes in cold water before cooking.

The lemon adds a delicious lightness of flavor to this unusual risotto. Use a good risotto rice such as arborio or carnaroli. Beating the risotto at the end of cooking—known as "mantecare" in Italian—gives this dish its lovely creamy quality. Serve it with freshly grated Parmesan cheese to sprinkle on top.

lemon, fennel, and mushroom risotto

2 tablespoons extra virgin olive oil

3 tablespoons unsalted butter

1 onion, finely chopped

1 bulb of fennel, trimmed and chopped, feathery tops reserved

1½ cups risotto rice

5½ cups hot chicken or vegetable stock

coarsely grated zest and freshly squeezed juice of 1 lemon

1 small bay leaf

a few sprigs of fresh tarragon

8 oz. button mushrooms, sliced

½ cup mascarpone cheese

¾ cup freshly grated Parmesan cheese

sea salt and freshly ground black pepper

SERVES 4–5

Put half the oil and half the butter in a deep skillet or a wide saucepan and heat until melted. Add the onion, fennel, and a pinch of salt, and cook very gently for about 10 minutes until soft, golden but not browned. Add the rice, stir around in the buttery juices and cook over medium heat for 2–3 minutes until the rice looks translucent.

Add about 1 cup of the hot stock and ½ teaspoon salt, then cook, stirring occasionally, over medium heat until the rice absorbs the liquid. Add half the lemon zest, the bay leaf, and tarragon and continue to cook, adding the stock in batches of ⅔–¾ cup at a time, stirring until each portion is absorbed, before adding the next. This should take about 18–20 minutes and the rice should be tender but still have an al dente 'bite' to it. Use a little hot water if you run out of stock before the rice has finished cooking. The risotto should be nicely moist but not soupily wet.

Meanwhile, heat the remaining butter and oil in a small skillet and cook the mushrooms over medium heat until tender but not browned. Turn up the heat and squeeze in the juice of half a lemon. Let the liquid evaporate, then take the mushrooms off the heat. As soon as the rice is cooked, beat in the mushrooms, mascarpone, most of the remaining lemon juice, and half the Parmesan. Add more lemon juice, salt, and pepper to taste. Cover, let rest for 3–4 minutes, then stir well and serve in warmed bowls, sprinkled with chopped fennel tops and the remaining lemon zest. Serve with the remaining Parmesan.

Seafood, such as mussels, clams, and shrimp, has its own sweetness that is always delicious with the sharpness of lemon. Together with gently cooked garlic and fiery red chile, this makes a classic sauce to toss through cooked pasta—use a thin pasta, such as spaghetti or linguine. There is no need to serve Parmesan with this dish.

pasta with mussels, shrimp, lemon, and garlic

2¼ lb. fresh mussels or clams, in the shell

½ cup white wine

1 shallot, finely chopped

14 oz. spaghetti

7 tablespoons extra virgin olive oil, plus extra to serve

¼ teaspoon dried red pepper flakes

1 garlic clove, finely chopped

12–14 oz. large uncooked shrimp, peeled and deveined, tails left on

1 teaspoon grated lemon zest

1 tablespoon freshly squeezed lemon juice, plus extra to taste

3 tablespoons finely chopped fresh flat-leaf parsley

sea salt and freshly ground black pepper

SERVES 4

Scrub the mussels thoroughly and discard any that still gape open after cleaning. Put the wine and shallot in a large saucepan, bring to the boil and simmer for a few minutes. Add the mussels, cover tightly, and cook over high heat for 4–5 minutes, shaking the pan 2 or 3 times, until all the mussels have opened. Drain, retaining the liquid and discard any mussels that haven't opened. Shell the mussels, retaining a few in the shell for serving.

Cook the spaghetti according to the package instructions in boiling salted water until just tender (9–11 minutes).

Meanwhile, put the oil in a wide pan over very low heat and let warm. Add the pepper flakes and cook gently for 2–3 minutes before adding the garlic. Keep the heat very low—the garlic should barely bubble and certainly not brown—and shake the pan from time to time. Allow about 5 minutes for the flavors to infuse the oil. Add the shrimp and cook gently until they turn pink and opaque, then put them on a plate. Add the mussel cooking liquid, lemon zest, and lemon juice to the pan and cook quickly to reduce by a few spoonfuls. Add the cooked mussels and shrimp to heat through.

When the pasta is ready, drain, then toss it immediately with the seafood and parsley, adding a little extra lemon juice to taste. Season with pepper and serve immediately in warmed bowls with a small bottle of olive oil to drizzle on top.

FISH, POULTRY, AND MEAT

Chermoula is a Moroccan spice paste or marinade that is fragrant with fresh cilantro, garlic, lemon, and spices. It is a particularly useful flavoring to have under your belt, as it is wonderfully adaptable, working equally well with fish, lamb, or chicken and marries well with many herbs. Grilling the lemon releases the juice and mellows its flavor, making it perfect for squeezing over the grilled fish.

2 whole fish, about 1½ lb. each, such as snapper, sea bass, sea bream, or grey mullet, scaled, cleaned, and fins trimmed

a few bay leaves

a few sprigs of fresh lemon thyme

2 tablespoons extra virgin olive oil, plus extra for basting

2 juicy lemons, halved

sea salt and freshly ground black pepper

CHERMOULA

1 teaspoon ground cumin

1 teaspoon ground coriander

a pinch of saffron threads

2 garlic cloves, chopped

1 teaspoon grated lemon zest

1 teaspoon mild paprika, preferably Spanish smoked pimentón

2 tablespoons chopped fresh flat-leaf parsley

3 tablespoons chopped fresh cilantro

freshly squeezed juice of 1 lemon

¼ cup extra virgin olive oil

cayenne or chile powder, to taste

SERVES 4

grilled fish with chermoula and grilled lemons

To make the chermoula, put the cumin, ground coriander, and saffron in a small saucepan and heat gently for 1 minute to release the aromas. Transfer to a small food processor or spice mill, then add the garlic, lemon zest, paprika, parsley, and cilantro and finely chop. Add the lemon juice and oil and blend to make a paste. Add a little cayenne or chile powder, salt, and pepper to taste, cover and set aside for 30 minutes.

Season the cavities of the fish with salt. Cut 4 or 5 diagonal, shallow slashes on each side of the fish and work a little chermoula into each cut. Lay the fish in a heatproof dish and stuff a few bay leaves and a little thyme into the cavities. Cover and let stand in the refrigerator for 30–60 minutes.

Season the fish with salt and pepper and sprinkle with the oil, then put under a preheated broiler, with the rack set about 4 inches from the heat. Broil for about 5 minutes on each side or until the fish is just cooked at the center— test with the tip of a pointed knife. When you turn the fish, add the lemon halves, cut side up, and baste them with a little extra oil. Broil until the cut surface of the lemons is nicely brown and the fish cooked. Serve the fish and lemons immediately with any remaining chermoula.

Note You can grill both fish and lemons. Use a special wire fish grilling cage or rack, which makes turning the fish easier. Oil the rack slightly so the skin doesn't stick and allow up to 10 minutes per side, depending on the heat of the coals and the size of the fish. Place the lemon halves directly on the barbecue or, alternatively, cook them on a ridged stovetop grill pan for 2–3 minutes until the cut surfaces are seared.

½ cup extra virgin olive oil

2 onions, halved and thinly sliced

2 garlic cloves, chopped

1–2 pinches of dried red pepper flakes

1 teaspoon crushed coriander seeds

½ teaspoon dried oregano

1½ lb. waxy-fleshed potatoes, peeled and cut into wedges

2 bay leaves

5 tablespoons white wine or vermouth

½ teaspoon grated lemon zest

1½ lb. white fish (on or off the bone), cut into large chunks or steaks

2 small lemons, halved

1 tablespoon chopped fresh oregano

1 tablespoon chopped fresh flat-leaf parsley

sea salt and freshly ground black pepper

a large skillet or skillet with lid

a large ovenproof baking dish

SERVES 4

If you have a stovetop-to-oven pan, this dish can be cooked all in one pot. Use chunks of white fish such as monkfish, cod, snapper, seabass, halibut, or haddock and choose potatoes that don't break up on cooking— large, waxy salad potatoes are ideal. As a rule of thumb, yellow-fleshed potatoes are waxy, while white potatoes tend to be floury. Some steamed greens tossed in a little olive oil make a great accompaniment to this dish.

fish baked with lemon, oregano, and potatoes

Heat a large skillet or ovenproof lidded skillet over medium heat and add the oil. Add the onion and sauté for 2–3 minutes, then turn the heat down low. Add 1–2 pinches of salt, cover, and let the onion cook very gently for 10–12 minutes until soft and golden yellow. Add the garlic, pepper flakes, crushed coriander seeds, and dried oregano. Cook for another 3–4 minutes.

Add the potatoes and bay leaves to the pan, turning them in the oily onions. Season with 1 teaspoon salt and several turns of the pepper mill, cook for a few minutes, then add the wine and lemon zest. When it bubbles, cover and cook gently for 15–20 minutes or until the potatoes are just tender.

Transfer the potatoes to a large ovenproof baking dish, if necessary. Season the fish with a little salt, then nestle the fish into the potatoes. Squeeze a little lemon juice from one of the lemon halves over the fish and spoon over a little of the oily juices. Add the lemon halves to the dish and turn in the oil.

Bake, uncovered, in a preheated oven at 400°F for 20–25 minutes, basting once or twice, until the potatoes are fully tender and the fish cooked through. The lemons should be touched with brown. Serve immediately, sprinkled with the fresh oregano and parsley.

The smell of roasting chicken, garlic, and herbs is indescribably delicious. The best kind of chicken to use is one with some character—organically raised to have some flavor and texture. However, you can also use a pair of guinea fowl or four poussins. The garlic cooks to a mellow softness and you eat it by squeezing it out of its skin onto the chicken. I'd serve it with boiled potatoes and a green vegetable.

roast lemon chicken
with garlic and herbs

4 lb. roasting chicken, at room temperature

5 tablespoons butter

1 teaspoon grated lemon zest

6 sprigs of French tarragon, about 2 inches long each

a small bunch of chervil, chopped

1 large onion, thickly sliced

1½–2 lemons

2 bay leaves

2 whole heads of garlic, halved crossways

1 tablespoon extra virgin olive oil

½ cup white wine or vermouth

1 cup chicken stock

1 teaspoon redcurrant or crabapple jelly

5–6 tablespoons heavy cream

sea salt and freshly ground black pepper

SERVES 4–5

Wash and dry the chicken and remove any trussing string or elastic. Cream the butter with the lemon zest and ½ teaspoon pepper. Chop 2 sprigs of tarragon and beat into the butter with half the chervil. Use your fingers to ease the skin of the chicken away from the breast meat. Spread most of the butter over the breast under the skin. Put the onion slices in an oiled roasting pan and sit the chicken on top. Season with salt and pepper. Cut 1 lemon in half and squeeze one half over the chicken, then put both halves in the cavity with any remaining butter, the bay leaves, and 2 sprigs of tarragon. Nestle the garlic halves around the chicken. Drizzle the garlic with the oil.

Cook in a preheated oven at 425°F for 30 minutes, then baste the chicken and garlic well with the juices, and spoon a little wine over the garlic. Cover loosely with foil and cook for another 50–60 minutes at 350°F. Uncover and baste the chicken for the last 15 minutes. Push a skewer into the thickest part of the chicken—if the juices run clear, it's done; if pink, give it another 10–15 minutes and test again.

Remove the chicken and garlic from the roasting pan and keep warm for 15–20 minutes, covered loosely with foil. Spoon off the excess fat from the roasting pan, then put the pan over medium-high heat and add the remaining wine. As it bubbles, stir in the fruit jelly, let it dissolve, then add the stock. Turn up the heat to high and let it bubble and reduce by about half, stirring to incorporate all the onion. Add the juice of half a lemon, then taste and add more if you like. Add the cream and let it bubble for a few seconds. Strain into a clean pan, then stir in the remaining tarragon, chopped, and chervil. Adjust the seasoning and serve immediately with the carved chicken.

1¾ lb. pork tenderloin

lime wedges, to serve

LIME AND GINGER MARINADE

grated zest of 1 lime

1 heaping teaspoon
grated fresh ginger

1 teaspoon ground coriander seeds

1 garlic clove, crushed

1 teaspoon honey or brown sugar

3 tablespoons plain yogurt

2 tablespoons extra virgin olive oil

16 fresh bay leaves

sea salt and freshly
ground black pepper

LIME AND PAPAYA SALSA

1 large papaya

3-inch piece of cucumber,
seeded and finely chopped

1 small red onion, finely chopped

4 oz. cherry tomatoes, halved

1 hot green chile, seeded
and finely chopped

½ teaspoon cumin seeds, toasted
in a dry skillet, then crushed,
plus extra to taste

grated zest of 1 lime

freshly squeezed juice of 1–2 limes

1–2 pinches of brown sugar

1–2 teaspoons Thai fish sauce

2 tablespoons chopped
fresh cilantro

*8 wooden skewers, soaked in
cold water and lightly oiled*

SERVES 4

*The lime and ginger marinade forms a delicious coating
for the pork, keeping it moist as it cooks. I like to serve
it with a spicy, sweet-savory salsa. The sharp lime and
sweet papaya is quite mouthwatering combined with
the hot, seared pork. A rice pilaf and a crisp green
salad would make a complete meal.*

grilled pork skewers

with lime and papaya salsa

To make the marinade, put the lime zest, ginger, ground coriander
seeds, garlic, honey or sugar, and yoghurt in a bowl, mix well,
then beat in 1 tablespoon of the oil. Season with salt and pepper.

Cut the pork into thin strips about 1 inch long and ¼ inch wide,
add to the marinade, then mix in the bay leaves. Cover and leave
to marinate in the refrigerator for 2–5 hours.

Meanwhile, to make the salsa, peel the papaya, scoop out the
seeds, and dice the flesh. Put in a non-metallic bowl with the
cucumber, onion, tomatoes, chile, crushed cumin seeds, and lime
zest and mix gently. Season to taste with lime juice, sugar, and
fish sauce. Cover and let stand for 20–30 minutes. Stir in the
remaining oil and the fresh cilantro and add more lime juice and/or
cumin, sugar, or fish sauce to taste.

Thread the pork, accordian-style, onto the presoaked skewers,
adding 2 bay leaves to each skewer. Cook on a preheated
outdoor grill or ridged stovetop grill pan for 4–5 minutes on each
side until cooked through, squeezing over a little lime juice as it
cooks. Serve the skewers with the salsa and lime wedges.

The lemon and herb mixture sprinkled over the pork at the end of cooking is known in Italy as gremolata. It adds a fresh burst of flavor to braised and roast meats. You need some pork with character for this easily put together dish—meat from organically raised pigs will have lots of flavor to match the powerful tastes of the aromatics. Serve with mashed potato or mashed celeriac and a green vegetable, such as buttered cabbage.

baked pork chops with lemon, garlic, and fennel

1–2 large garlic cloves

1 teaspoon fennel seeds

2 teaspoons grated lemon zest

2 tablespoons extra virgin olive oil

4 meaty pork loin chops on the bone

2 large bulbs of fennel, trimmed and cut into wedges, feathery tops reserved

5 garlic cloves, unpeeled

½ cup white vermouth

2–4 bay leaves

1–2 pinches of sugar

1 small lemon, halved

sea salt and freshly ground black pepper

a shallow ovenproof baking dish

SERVES 4

Using a mortar and pestle, crush the garlic with the fennel seeds and ¼ teaspoon salt, then work in half the lemon zest and 1 tablespoon of the oil. Rub the mixture all over the chops in a non-metallic dish, cover and leave to marinate, in the refrigerator for 2–8 hours.

Scrape the marinade off the pork and reserve. Heat a skillet and brown the chops over medium-high heat for about 2–3 minutes on each side. Transfer to a shallow ovenproof baking dish.

Reduce the heat, add the remaining oil and lightly brown the fennel wedges on each side. Add 4 of the garlic cloves to the pan, the vermouth and the reserved marinade and let bubble for 3–4 minutes. Add ½ cup water and the bay leaves and let bubble gently until the liquid has reduced by half and the fennel is just tender. Add salt, pepper and sugar to taste, then pour over the chops, nestling in the fennel. Squeeze over a little lemon juice from one of the lemon wedges, then nestle the lemon wedges into the pork.

Bake, uncovered, in a preheated oven at 400°F for 30–35 minutes, spooning over the juices once or twice as it cooks.

To make the gremolata, chop the remaining garlic clove and fennel tops together, then mix in a bowl with the remaining lemon zest. Sprinkle over the pork and serve immediately.

There's a Mexican feel to the spices and bold flavors of this beef dish. Serve with either rice and wilted greens or soft wheat tortillas, crisp salad, and a sour cream herb dip. The cilantro lime relish works particularly well with the smoky flavors of the beef and mushrooms, and the sweetness of the potatoes, but it's also good with grilled pork or chicken or seared tuna and swordfish.

1 teaspoon cumin seeds, crushed

1 teaspoon grated lime zest

¼ teaspoon dried red pepper flakes

1½–1¾ lb. rump or sirloin steak, trimmed of excess fat

4 sweet potatoes, unpeeled

4 large flat portobello mushrooms

¼ cup extra virgin olive oil

freshly squeezed juice of 1 lime

2 tablespoons chopped cilantro

sea salt and freshly ground black pepper

CILANTRO LIME RELISH

1 red onion, thinly sliced

freshly squeezed juice of 1–2 limes

1–2 teaspoons sugar

grated zest of ½ lime

½ teaspoon crushed cumin seeds, toasted in a dry skillet

2 large vine-ripened tomatoes, chopped, about ½ lb.

1–2 hot green chiles, seeded and finely chopped

2–3 tablespoons chopped cilantro

SERVES 4

seared beef with lime and cumin rub, sweet potatoes,

and cilantro lime relish

Put the crushed cumin seeds, lime zest, pepper flakes, and ¼ teaspoon pepper in a small bowl and mix well. Rub the mixture over the steak, cover and leave to marinate in the refrigerator for 2–8 hours. Bring to room temperature before cooking. Par-boil the sweet potatoes in boiling water for 6–8 minutes. Drain, let cool, and cut into ½-inch slices.

To make the relish, put the onion in a sieve and pour over a kettle of boiling water. Drain, run under the cold tap and drain well. Pat dry with paper towels, then put in a non-metallic bowl with the juice of 1 lime, 1 teaspoon sugar, lime zest, and cumin seeds and toss well. Stir in the tomatoes, chiles, and cilantro. Cover and set aside for 20–30 minutes, then add salt, sugar and/or lime juice to taste.

Heat a ridged stovetop grill pan until hot and sear the steak on both sides—5 minutes on each side will make a thick steak medium-rare. Season with salt and keep warm covered loosely with foil.

Brush the sweet potato slices and mushrooms with oil and season with salt and pepper. Cook on the grill pan for 4–5 minutes each side, squeezing some of the lime juice over the mushrooms as they finish cooking. Slice the mushrooms and toss with any remaining oil, lime juice to taste, and the chopped cilantro. Season with salt and pepper and put on dinner plates. Slice the steak thickly and arrange on top of the vegetables. Serve with the relish.

This Moroccan-style stew is heady with spices, herbs, and dried fruit, but it is the preserved lemon that gives that essential North African flavor. You don't need much, but once you have a taste for it, its mellowed sharpness is almost addictive. Serve with either a saffron-scented rice pilaf or couscous to soak up the delicious juices.

moroccan lamb tagine with preserved lemons and carrots

1¾ lb. boneless shoulder of lamb, trimmed of excess fat and cut into 2 inch cubes

1 recipe Chermoula (page 23)

3 tablespoons extra virgin olive oil

1 large onion, halved and thinly sliced

2 garlic cloves, finely chopped

4 large sun-ripened tomatoes, peeled, seeded, and chopped, 12–14 oz.

2 cups lamb or vegetable stock

2 bay leaves

2 green bell peppers, seeded and thickly sliced

2 lbs. carrots, thickly sliced

6 oz. prunes or dried apricots

½–1 Preserved Lemon (page 61), chopped

TO SERVE

2 tablespoons chopped fresh cilantro

1 teaspoon grated lemon zest

SERVES 4

Put the lamb and half the chermoula in a non-metallic bowl, toss well to coat, then cover and let marinate in the refrigerator for 2–12 hours (keep the remaining chermoula in the refrigerator too, tightly covered).

Scrape the chermoula off the lamb and reserve in a small bowl, then heat 2 tablespoons of the oil in a large skillet. Add the meat, in batches if necessary, and brown on all sides over medium-high heat. Put the meat in a casserole as it browns.

Heat the remaining oil in the skillet, add the onion, and cook gently for 10–15 minutes until softened and just beginning to brown. Add the garlic and the chermoula marinade from the lamb and cook for a few more minutes over medium heat. Add the tomatoes and cook for another 5 minutes. Add the stock and bay leaves and let simmer for a few minutes, then pour over the lamb. Season with salt and pepper, cover tightly and cook in a preheated oven at 350°F for 1 hour.

Uncover, then stir in the green pepper, carrots, and prunes or apricots. Add up to ½ cup water (or extra stock) if the stew seems dry. Cover and cook for another 50–60 minutes, when the carrots and lamb should be tender. Test and cook for another 15–20 minutes if necessary.

Stir in the remaining chermoula and the preserved lemon and let it heat through for 5 minutes. Add salt and pepper to taste, then serve sprinkled with the cilantro and lemon zest.

8 oz. digestive biscuits
or graham crackers

2 tablespoons sugar

2 teaspoons ground ginger

1 stick unsalted butter, melted

CHEESECAKE FILLING

20 oz. cream cheese

1 cup sugar

1 tablespoon cornstarch

4 large eggs, beaten

grated zest of 2 lemons

1½ cups sour cream

GINGER TOPPING

1 cup sour cream

2½ tablespoons sugar

2½ oz. stem ginger in syrup,
drained and finely chopped

finely grated zest of 1 lemon

*a springform cake pan,
10 inches diameter*

*a roasting pan to fit the cake pan
in comfortably*

SERVES 8–10

The water-bath method for cooking cheesecakes is quite well known now, thanks to cookery writers like Rose Levy Beranbaum and Nigella Lawson. It is quite simply the best way of producing a silky smooth, velvety-textured cheesecake that melts on the tongue.

lemon and ginger cheesecake

First prepare the cake pan. Cover the outside of the pan with a double layer of foil, molding it to the pan, but being careful not to puncture it so that it remains watertight. Line the base of the pan with a piece of baking paper.

Put the biscuits in a food processor and pulse to form fine crumbs. Add the sugar and ground ginger and blend again. Transfer to a bowl and stir in the melted butter until evenly mixed. Spoon the crumbs into the prepared pan and press down to form an even layer on the base and sides of the pan. Bake in a preheated oven at 350°F for 10–12 minutes to set the crust, then let cool.

To make the filling, put the cream cheese and sugar in a large bowl and beat until smooth. Beat in the cornstarch, followed by the eggs in about 4 portions. When smooth, beat in the lemon zest and sour cream. Pour the mixture over the crumb base. Set the cake pan in the roasting pan and pour very hot water into the roasting pan to come just over half-way up the sides of the cake pan. Transfer the pans to the oven and bake, at the same temperature, for 45–50 minutes or until the mixture is just set in the center.

Meanwhile, to make the ginger topping, put the sour cream and 2 tablespoons of the sugar in a bowl and mix well. Take the cheesecake out of the oven and carefully spread the sour cream mixture over the surface. Sprinkle the chopped ginger evenly over the whole surface, then return to the oven for 10 minutes. Remove the cheesecake from its water bath, let cool on a wire rack, then chill, preferably overnight, before removing the foil and unmolding the cheesecake. Toss the grated lemon zest with the remaining sugar and use to decorate the cheesecake just before serving.

SWEET THINGS

A classic French tarte au citron is perhaps the most famous, and most blissful, of all lemony sweet things. As with all classic recipes, many different versions abound, some require whole eggs, others an heroic number of egg yolks. Heresy though it may be, I think it's possible to make this tart too rich, so that the egginess overwhelms the sharpness of the lemon.

classic tarte au citron

1 recipe Sweet Tart Pastry (page 63)

2 large eggs, plus 4 egg yolks

1⅓ cups sugar

finely grated zest of 2 lemons

freshly squeezed juice of 5 lemons

1 cup heavy cream

¼ cup sour cream or crème fraîche

¼ cup sifted confectioners' sugar or granulated sugar, to glaze

a loose-based metal flan tin, 10–12 inches diameter, about 1 inch deep

a cook's blowtorch (optional)

SERVES 8–10

Roll out the pastry thinly and use to line the flan tin. Bake blind following the method given on page 63.

Put the eggs and egg yolks in a bowl and beat well until thoroughly blended but not frothy. Beat in the sugar, followed by the lemon zest. Gradually beat in the lemon juice, followed by the heavy cream and sour cream.

Carefully pour the filling into the pastry case and bake in a preheated oven at 325°F for 35–40 minutes. The center of the tart should just wobble a little when the tart is pushed. Let cool on a wire rack in the tin. Remove the tart from the tin when cool.

Dust with the confectioners' sugar or granulated sugar, then caramelize using with a cook's blowtorch. Alternatively, protect the edge of the pastry with foil strips and put the tart under a very hot broiler for 1–2 minutes until the sugar melts and browns (you may have to move the tart around to achieve an even color). Let the tart cool and serve cold, but do not chill.

Passionfruit makes a deliciously different take on the more familiar lemon curd; at once tart, sweet, and perfumed with an exotic fragrance. Make these tarts small—petit four size, really—so that they form mouthfuls of crisp sweet pastry that set off the intense fruitiness and butteriness of the filling.

passionfruit and lime curd tarts

thinly pared zest of 2 limes

¼ cup granulated sugar

1½ cups Passionfruit and Lime Curd (page 62)

confectioners' sugar, to dust

CARDAMOM AND LIME PASTRY

1 stick unsalted butter, softened

¼ cup confectioners' sugar, sifted

1 egg yolk

¼ teaspoon ground cardamom

1 teaspoon finely grated lime zest

1¼ cups plain flour, plus extra as necessary

1 tablespoon cornstarch

a pinch of sea salt

a 24-hole tartlet tray

MAKES 24 SMALL TARTLETS

To make the pastry, cream the butter and confectioners' sugar together until fluffy, then beat in the egg yolk, followed by the cardamom and lime zest. Sift the flours and salt together and work into the mixture, adding a teaspoon or so of extra flour as necessary to make a smooth but not sticky dough. Form into a smooth ball, wrap in foil, and chill in the refrigerator for at least 1 hour.

Take the dough out of the refrigerator and let it soften for 5–10 minutes. Roll out thinly on a well-floured work surface. Cut out rounds and use to line the tartlet tray. Chill for 5–10 minutes, prick the bases with a fork, then bake in a preheated oven at 375°F for 10–15 minutes until pale biscuit brown. Check frequently as they burn easily in the final minutes. Let cool on a wire rack.

Meanwhile, to make the candied lime zest, put the lime zest in a heatproof bowl and cover with boiling water. Let stand for 2 minutes, drain and then repeat. Leave to drain. Put the granulated sugar in a small pan with 5 tablespoons water over low heat and stir until the sugar dissolves. Add the lime zest, bring to the boil, then simmer gently for 6–8 minutes until the syrup is sticky and the lime looks candied. Remove the zest with a fork and put on a tray lined with a piece of nonstick baking paper or foil.

Fill the tartlet cases with teaspoonfuls of the Passionfruit and Lime Curd. Top with a few shreds of candied lime zest and lightly dust with icing sugar. Serve immediately.

One of my earliest cooking memories as a child was making lemon meringue pie, using a packet mix for the filling and waiting for the little gelatine capsule of "lemon" flavor to miraculously burst. Happy days, but now I prefer this buttery, lemony filling for my pie. The cloud of fluffy, crisp-crusted meringue is still mandatory, however, for any lemon meringue pie worthy of the name.

lemon meringue pie

1 recipe Sweet Tart Pastry (page 63)

LEMON FILLING

1 large egg and 3 large eggs yolks

½ cup sugar

finely grated zest and freshly squeezed juice of 2 large lemons

1 stick unsalted butter, melted and cooled

½ cup whipping cream

MERINGUE

3 large egg whites

¼ teaspoon cream of tartar

½ cup sugar, plus 1 tablespoon

½ teaspoon finely grated lemon zest

a 9–10 inch loose-bottomed tart tin

SERVES 6–8

Roll out the pastry and use to line the tart tin. Bake blind following the method given on page 63.

Put the egg, egg yolks, and sugar in a bowl and beat until slightly thickened and a paler yellow. Beat in the lemon zest, butter, cream, and finally the lemon juice. Pour the filling into the pastry case and bake in a preheated oven at 325°F for 20–30 minutes until the filling is barely set in the center. Do not let it overbake.

To make the meringue, put the egg whites and cream of tartar in a grease-free bowl and, using an electric whisk, whisk until frothy and the whisk leaves stiff peaks. Whisk in half the sugar until the meringue is thick and glossy. Fold in the remaining sugar and the lemon zest using a metal spoon. Pile the meringue onto the tart, swirling and peaking as you go. Sprinkle with the 1 tablespoon sugar and return the tart to the oven for another 30–35 minutes or until the meringue is browned and crisp on the outside. Serve just warm or cold.

Variation You can make a very easy lemon (or indeed lime) meringue pie by filling the pastry case with Lemon Curd (page 62) or Lime and Cardamom Curd (page 62), then topping with the meringue and baking as above.

This classic dessert originates from the Florida Keys where limes were once grown plentifully. You may well be apprehensive about using condensed milk in this recipe, but don't be; the sharp lime juice counters the intense sweetness, yielding a tangy but deeply satisfying creamy filling.

key lime pie

1 recipe Sweet Tart Pastry (page 63)

LIME FILLING

4 eggs, separated

one 14-oz. can sweetened condensed milk

2 tablespoons grated lime zest

½ cup, plus 1 tablespoon freshly squeezed lime juice (5–6 limes)

¼ teaspoon cream of tartar

CREAM TOPPING

1 cup whipping cream

3 tablespoons vanilla sugar*

zest of 1 large lime, pared into fine shreds

a tart tin, 10 inches diameter

SERVES 6–8

Roll out the pastry and use to line the tart tin. Bake blind following the method given on page 63.

To make the lime filling, put 1 whole egg and 3 egg yolks in a bowl and beat until blended. Whisk in the condensed milk and lime zest. Gradually whisk in the lime juice.

Put the egg whites and cream of tartar in a separate, grease-free bowl and whisk until stiff but not dry. Beat 2 tablespoons of egg white mixture into the egg yolk mixture, then fold in the remainder with a spatula. Scrape into the pastry case and bake in a preheated oven at 350°F for about 20 minutes or until risen and just firm in the center. Remove from the oven and let cool in its tin on a wire rack. It will deflate as it cools.

When cool, make the topping. Put the cream and 2 tablespoons of the sugar in a bowl, whip until softly stiff, then spread over the lime filling. Toss the shreds of lime zest in the remaining sugar and use to decorate the tart. Serve cold but not chilled.

*Note To make the vanilla sugar, bury 2 or 3 vanilla beans in a jar of sugar and leave for 1 week, after which the sugar will take on the aroma of vanilla. Or, for a quick version, grind 3 tablespoons sugar with a small piece of vanilla bean in a clean coffee grinder.

Variation You can also use a biscuit pie crust for a Key Lime Pie. Follow the directions in the recipe for the Lemon and Ginger Cheesecake (page 36), omitting the ground ginger.

I'm not a huge fan of either lemon or lime with dark chocolate, as the fruitiness of good chocolate is cancelled out by the citrus flavor. However, the sharpness of lime cuts through the creamy sweetness of white chocolate deliciously in this dreamy dessert, shot through with the citrus flavor of cardamom. Make sure you use freshly ground, inky-black cardamom seeds.

lime, white chocolate, and cardamom tartlets

1 recipe Sweet Tart Pastry (page 63)

2 large eggs, plus 2 large egg yolks

½ cup sugar

finely grated zest and freshly squeezed juice of 4 limes

1 cup heavy cream

3½ oz. good-quality white chocolate

½ cup plus 1 tablespoon sour cream

¼ teaspoon freshly ground cardamom seeds

3 oz. bittersweet chocolate

confectioners' sugar, to dust

6 tartlet tins, 3 inches diameter

SERVES 6–8

Roll out the pastry and use to line the tartlet tins. Prick the bases with a fork and bake blind following the method given on page 63.

Put the eggs, egg yolks, and sugar in a bowl and beat until blended but not frothy. Gradually whisk in the lime zest, followed by the lime juice and finally the cream. Pour the mixture into the pastry cases and bake in a preheated oven at 350°F for 20–25 minutes or until just set in the center (it will continue to firm up as it cools). Remove from the oven and let cool in their tins.

Meanwhile, break the white chocolate into a heatproof bowl and add the sour cream and ground cardamom seeds. Place the bowl over a saucepan of barely simmering water and stir frequently until the chocolate melts and the mixture becomes smooth. Cool, stirring from time to time, then spread the chocolate mixture over the lime filling.

Melt the dark chocolate as above and stir until smooth. Make a parchment paper cone, spoon in the chocolate, fold over to seal, then cut off the tip of the cone. Drizzle in criss-cross zigzags over the tartlets or pipe shapes onto nonstick paper. Chill the tartlets until the chocolate sets, then decorate with the chocolate shapes, if necessary. Unmold and dust with confectioners' sugar just before serving.

Variation Alternatively, you can bake one large tart. Roll out the pastry and use to line a 10-inch loose-based tart tin. Bake blind following the method on page 63.

This delightfully fresh-tasting dessert is based on a traditional British recipe. Served warm (truthfully, it's best that way), the bottom layer forms a tangy, lemony sauce for the light sponge layer, but it is also delicious cold (see Variation), when the sauce sets into a light custard that is lovely with the taste of blackberries. So there you are—two recipes for the price of one!

lemon and blackberry puddings

6–8 oz. ripe blackberries

½ cup superfine sugar, plus 1 tablespoon

½ stick butter, softened

1 vanilla bean

grated zest and freshly squeezed juice of 1 large lemon

2 large eggs, separated

2 slightly heaping tablespoons flour

1 cup milk

4 tablespoons whipping cream, plus extra to serve

½ teaspoon cream of tartar

4–5 small ovenproof dishes, buttered

SERVES 4–5

Put the blackberries and the 1 tablespoon sugar in a bowl, toss gently, then spoon into the dishes.

Put the butter and the remaining sugar in a bowl and beat until creamy. Split the vanilla bean, scrape the seeds into the mixture and beat to mix. Beat in the lemon zest, followed by the egg yolks. Sift in the flour, stir in, then gradually beat in the milk, cream, and lemon juice.

Put the egg whites and cream of tartar in a separate, grease-free bowl and whisk until stiff but not dry. Beat 2 tablespoons of the egg whites into the pudding mixture, then fold in the remainder with a spatula. Spoon the mixture into the prepared dishes and bake in a preheated oven at 350°F for 30–35 minutes. Serve hot or warm, with cold cream, if you like.

Variation To serve cold, bake in a 1 quart shallow ovenproof dish for an additional 5–10 minutes. Let cool (it will sink and deflate), then chill. When ready to serve, whisk 1 scant cup whipping cream and 2 tablespoons vanilla sugar (page 44) in a bowl until billowy and thick. Spread the cream over the pudding, then decorate with extra blackberries and strips of lemon zest.

Cooking brings out the flavor of blueberries, which can be a rather uneventful fruit when eaten raw. Here, they pepper a light butter cake flavored with lime zest, then the whole thing is drenched in lime syrup, which soaks into the cake to add flavor and moistness. It is ideal to take on a picnic or to serve as a special dessert, because it tastes even better when made a day ahead.

lime and blueberry cake with lime syrup

1 stick plus 6 tablespoons unsalted butter, softened

1 cup plus 3 tablespoons natural cane sugar

4 eggs, beaten

1¾ cups self-raising flour, sifted with a pinch of sea salt

1 pint blueberries

grated zest of 2 limes

3 tablespoons ground almonds

1–2 teaspoons limes

LIME SYRUP

freshly squeezed juice of 4 limes

grated zest of 1 lime

½ cup plus 1 tablespoon natural cane sugar

a solid-based cake pan, 9–10 inches square, buttered and lined with buttered parchment paper

MAKES 12 SQUARES

Put the butter and sugar in a bowl and beat until light. Gradually beat in the eggs, adding a little of the flour towards the end to prevent curdling. Toss the blueberries with 1 tablespoon of the remaining flour and set aside. Beat the lime zest into the cake mixture, then fold in the remaining flour and almonds. Fold in 1–2 teaspoons lime juice to give you a good dropping consistency—the mixture should drop easily from the spoon when tapped.

Fold in most of the blueberries (about 1½ cups) and transfer to the prepared cake pan. Smooth down, then sprinkle with the remaining fruit (which will sink as the cake rises). Bake in a preheated oven at 350°F for about 40–45 minutes or until firm to a gentle touch in the center.

While the cake is cooking, make the syrup. Put the lime juice, zest, and sugar in a small saucepan, heat gently and stir. Do not let it bubble—just heat slightly, leaving a slight graininess. Immediately the cake comes out of the oven, prick it all over with a skewer, then spoon over the syrup. Let the cake cool in its pan.

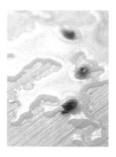

The aromatic sharpness of lime and the heat of chile bring out the sweetness and scented flavor of exotic fruits such as papaya, mango, and pineapple. Even starfruit, a pretty but often uninspiring fruit, yields to this treatment. I'd serve this with a scoop of good vanilla ice cream, or one infused with the citrus taste of cardamom. A lime sorbet would also work well.

tropical fruits in lime and chile syrup

1 large ripe papaya

1 large ripe mango

1 ripe pineapple

2 starfruit or kiwis, thinly sliced

LIME AND CHILE SYRUP

½ cup sugar

thinly pared zest of 2 limes

freshly squeezed juice of up to 1 lime

1 mild to hot green or red chile, seeded and finely diced

SERVES 6

To make the syrup, put the sugar and ½ cup water in a small saucepan over low heat and stir to dissolve the sugar.

Meanwhile, put the shreds of lime zest in a heatproof bowl and cover with boiling water. Let stand for 5 minutes, drain and repeat, then drain well.

When the sugar has dissolved, boil the syrup for 3–4 minutes until it thickens slightly, but do not let it burn. Let cool a little, then stir in the lime zest, followed by sufficient lime juice to make a sweet-sour syrup. Add about 1 teaspoon chile and set aside. Taste after 10 minutes and add more chile to taste, but remember that the chile will get hotter as the syrup cools.

To prepare the fruits, peel and destone the papaya and cut into slices. Peel, seed, and slice the mango. Peel, core, and thinly slice the pineapple. Arrange all the fruit on a platter or on individual plates. Trickle the syrup over the top, cover, and chill for at least 30 minutes before serving.

Nothing says high summer more than a perfect, juicy ripe peach—the kind it's impossible to eat without getting juice all over your chin and fingers. Unfortunately, peaches like that are all too rare, but a little warmth, sugar and flavorings such as lemon, bay, and real vanilla can transform the most lackluster fruit into something headily delicious.

peaches in lemon, bay, and vanilla syrup

1¾ cup sugar

1 vanilla bean, split

3 fresh bay leaves

3 strips of lemon zest from 1 lemon

1–2 tablespoons freshly squeezed lemon juice

6 ripe white or yellow peaches, halved and pitted

SERVES 6

Put the sugar in a saucepan with 2½ cups water and heat gently, stirring all the time to dissolve the sugar. Add the vanilla bean, bay leaves, and the strips of lemon zest.

Let the syrup simmer for 5 minutes, then slip in the peaches, cut side up. Poach them gently (the liquid should merely bubble occasionally) for 5–8 minutes. Test them with the tip of a pointed knife. Remove the peaches carefully with a slotted spoon and, when cool enough, slip off the skin.

Meanwhile, reduce the liquid by fast boiling until it thickens slightly and becomes syrupy. Add the lemon juice to taste. Let cool, then pour the syrup over the peaches, tucking in the vanilla bean, bay leaves, and lemon zest. When cold, cover and chill.

Variation Oven-roasted Peaches with Lemon Sugar

Put 6 ripe peaches in a heatproof bowl and cover with boiling water. Leave for 30–60 seconds, then drain. Peel (the skins should come off easily), halve and stone. Place them in a lightly buttered ovenproof dish in one layer. Mix the grated zest of 1 lemon with ½ cup vanilla sugar (page 44) and scatter over the peaches, then put a knob of butter in each peach cavity. Squeeze over the juice of 1 lemon. Cook in a preheated oven at 400°F for 30–35 minutes, basting with the buttery juices once or twice. Serve warm with vanilla ice cream.

You can experiment with different flavors with this delightfully elegant herby sorbet, based on the recipe for tea sorbet in Caroline Liddell and Robin Weir's definitive book "Ices". Try Earl Grey tea with lemon balm or jasmine tea with lemon and ginger. The wafers go well with all kinds of ice creams and sorbets.

3 green tea tea bags

1 cup sugar

1 tablespoon thyme sprigs, preferably lemon thyme

thinly pared zest of 2 lemons

freshly squeezed juice of up to 1½ lemons

1 egg white, lightly beaten (optional)

PISTACHIO AND LEMON WAFERS

1 stick unsalted butter, softened

½ cup vanilla sugar (page 44)

grated zest of 1 lemon

1 egg, beaten

1½ cups flour

2 tablespoons potato flour or cornstarch

a pinch of sea salt

3½ oz. shelled, unsalted pistachio nuts, blanched and chopped

an ice cream maker (optional)

2 heavy baking sheets, buttered

SERVES 6–8

lemon, thyme, and green tea sorbet

with pistachio and lemon wafers

Place the tea bags in a bowl and pour over 2 cups cold water, cover, and leave overnight. The next day, dissolve the sugar in 1 cup water in a saucepan over low heat and bring to the boil. Take off the heat and pour into a heatproof bowl, then add the thyme and lemon zest. Let the syrup cool, cover, then chill in the refrigerator overnight.

The next day, strain both mixtures into a bowl or jug and stir in lemon juice to taste. Chill, then churn in an ice cream maker according to the manufacturer's instructions, and then freeze. If making by hand, turn into a freezerproof container to make a shallow layer and freeze until hard around the edges. Turn into a food processor, add the egg white and process until smooth. Repeat the freezing and beating once more, then allow to freeze firm.

To make the wafers, cream the butter and sugar until light. Beat in the lemon zest, then the egg. Sift in the flours and salt, then stir in the pistachios. Form the dough into a roll shape, approximately 2 inches in diameter, then put it in the center of a sheet of waxed paper. Roll up the paper to enclose the roll of dough, then chill until firm, at least 3 hours or overnight.

Using a sharp knife, cut off thin slices from the dough, 1 inch thick, and lay on the baking sheets. Bake in a preheated oven at 350°F for 12–15 minutes until browned around the edges. Let cool on a wire rack.

Let the sorbet soften in the refrigerator for 15–20 minutes, then serve with a few wafers for each person. Store the remaining wafers in an airtight tin.

This really is a very simple ice cream and yet also very delicious. Use homemade curd or, at a pinch, the very best bought stuff. I like it served quite plainly, though a spoonful of Italian Limoncello poured over each bowlful is heavenly. It also goes very well with strawberries, tossed in a little sugar and a few drops of lemon juice.

lemon curd ice cream

1 recipe Lemon Curd (page 62)

1 cup whipping or heavy cream

3 tablespoons confectioners' sugar, sifted

freshly squeezed lemon juice, to taste (optional)

SERVES 4–6

Beat the curd smooth in a bowl, then lightly whip the cream until it just begins to thicken and leave a whisk trail. Sweeten the cream with the sugar, then fold the cream into the curd. Sharpen the taste with lemon juice, if you like. Turn into a freezerproof container and freeze for at least 3 hours before serving. Alternatively, churn in an ice cream maker until softly frozen, following the manufacturer's instructions. Transfer to a freezerproof container and freeze until hard, 1–1½ hours, before serving.

Variations For a more unusual flavor, try using Lime and Cardomom Curd (page 62) or Passionfruit and Lime Curd (page 62) instead of lemon curd.

Lemon Meringue Ice Cream

Remove the ice cream from the freezer halfway through the freezing process (allow 1½–2 hours) and stir the mixture. Stir in some crumbled meringue, leaving some of the meringue in quite large chunks. Continue to freeze, as above.

BASICS

Serving a glass of chilled homemade lemonade on a sweltering summer's day conjures up images of Edwardian house parties and Merchant Ivory films—all white muslin, cucumber sandwiches, and faithful kitchen staff beavering away in the background. But fresh lemonade is simple to make, and if you keep the lemony syrup in the refrigerator, you have an almost instant drink to dilute with either chilled sparkling mineral water or soda water.

homemade fresh lemonade

thinly pared zest and
freshly squeezed juice of
6 large juicy lemons

1 cup white sugar

sparkling mineral water or soda
water, chilled, to dilute

TO SERVE

ice cubes

fresh lemon slices

sprigs of fresh mint

SERVES 6–8

Put the lemon zest, sugar, and 2½ cups water in a non-aluminum saucepan and bring slowly to a simmer, stirring to dissolve the sugar. As soon as the sugar is dissolved and the syrup begins to bubble, take it off the heat. Half cover and leave until cold.

Squeeze the lemons and add the juice to the cold syrup. Strain into a bowl or jug, cover and chill.

Serve in a glass jug with ice cubes, fresh lemon slices, and sprigs of mint, diluted with chilled sparkling mineral water or soda water on a ratio of about 1 part syrup to 1 part water.

Variations A Spanish cook I knew used to add saffron to her lemonade to make a startlingly golden-hued drink with an intriguing, refreshing taste. Just add a small pinch of saffron threads to the warm syrup when you take it off the heat.

Ginger and Limeade

Use the zest of 8 large limes and add a 2-inch piece of peeled fresh ginger, cut into fine slices, to infuse in the hot syrup. As limes are less juicy and sharper than lemons, you need the juice of about 10–12 fruit—allow 1½–1¾ cups juice to taste.

There are two methods of making this preserve (which can also be made with limes). The first is to preserve whole lemons in salt and lemon juice. The second, popularized by Middle Eastern food expert Claudia Roden, is to cover salted lemon slices with olive oil and a little paprika. The first method has a sharp and tangy flavor, while the second makes a more mellow, amber-colored preserve. Both preserves will keep for 6 months once opened.

preserved lemons *in sea salt*

14–15 small, fine-skinned lemons, thoroughly washed, plus extra lemon juice as necessary

½ cup sea salt, plus 2 tablespoons

1 tablespoon sugar

MAKES A 1 QUART JAR

Pack as many lemons into a sterilized 1 quart jar as you can, probably about 8 or 9. Take them out, put them in a bowl with the 2 tablespoons salt and pour cold water over to cover. Keep the lemons submerged with a plate and leave for 24 hours. Drain and dry.

Make two deep lengthways cuts into each soaked lemon and pack 1 teaspoon salt into each lemon. Sterilize the jar, then sprinkle a thin layer of salt on the base. Pack in the lemons, sprinkling in the remaining salt and sugar as you go. Press the lemons down hard. Squeeze the juice from the remaining lemons and strain it over the lemons in the jar to cover—it is important that the lemons are completely covered in liquid. Cover with plastic wrap or waxed paper then seal tightly. Leave for 1 week in a cool, dark spot, shaking the jar every day. Store in a dark, cool place for at least 4 weeks before using.

preserved lemons *in olive oil*

6 large lemons, thoroughly washed and thinly sliced

3 tablespoons sea salt

1½ teaspoons paprika, preferably Spanish pimentón

2 small dried red chiles (optional)

2–4 small fresh bay leaves

up to 3 cups mild olive oil (not extra virgin) or half sunflower and half mild olive oil

MAKES 2 X PINT JARS

Lay the lemon slices on trays in a single layer and sprinkle the salt over them, then freeze overnight. The following day, let them thaw and drain off the juices. Dab dry with kitchen paper.

Layer the lemon slices in 2 sterilized jars, sprinkling a little paprika between the layers. Add a chile to each jar, if using, and tuck 1–2 bay leaves down the side. Cover to at least ½-inch depth with the oil. Leave for 30 minutes, then tap several times on the work surface to dispel any air bubbles. Cover with plastic wrap or waxed paper, then seal tightly. Store in a dark, cool place for at least 4 weeks before using.

This is a quintessentially British preserve, tart with lemon yet sweet and buttery at the same time. It is delicious on toast or on freshly made scones or bread and also an excellent filling for tarts, sponge cakes, or meringues. Small jars make a great gift. It is very easy to make so long as you stir it very frequently as it cooks and keep the heat low so that the water in the pan barely bubbles. This will keep for 15 days in the refrigerator.

2 large lemons

1 stick unsalted butter, cut into cubes

1 cup sugar

3 eggs, beaten

MAKES 2 SMALL JARS, 8 OZ. EACH

lemon curd

Finely grate the zest from the lemons into a heatproof bowl. Squeeze the juice and add that to the bowl with the butter and sugar.

Place the bowl over a pan of just-simmering water, making sure the water doesn't touch the base of the bowl. Stir until the butter melts. Add the egg and, using a wooden spoon, stir the mixture over a gentle heat for 10–15 minutes until the mixture thickens noticeably and takes on a translucent look.

For a very smooth preserve, strain the curd through a fine sieve into a measuring cup, then pot it into small, sterilized, jars (page 4). Cover with plastic wrap or waxed paper when cold.

Variations Lime and Cardamom Curd

Substitute the zest of 3 large limes and the freshly squeezed juice of 5 limes for the lemons above. Add ¼ teaspoon finely ground cardamom seeds to the butter and sugar as it melts

Passionfruit and Lime Curd

Use the zest of 1 large lime, the freshly squeezed juice of 2 limes and the seived pulp of 8 ripe passionfruit (heating the pulp gently in the microwave for a few seconds makes it easier to sieve). Add 1–2 teaspoons of the passionfruit seeds at the end for crunch.

This pastry is easily made in a food processor and creates a crisp, biscuity crust that is great for sweet flans, pies, and tartlet cases. Don't be tempted to stint on the chilling—it makes the pastry much easier to roll out. Brushing the pastry with egg white as it cooks ensures a crisp finish and stops it becoming "soggy".

1⅓ cups flour

a pinch of salt

⅓ cup confectioners' sugar

6 tablespoons unsalted butter, chilled and cut into small cubes

1 large egg, separated

1½–2 tablespoons cold lemon juice or ice water

a loose-based tart tin, 9–10 inches diameter, 1–2 inches deep

MAKES 1 TART CASE, 9–10 INCHES DIAMETER

sweet tart pastry

Put the flour, salt, sugar, and butter in a food processor fitted with a metal blade. Process until the ingredients are thoroughly mixed and the mixture has a sandy appearance. Add the egg yolk and 1½ tablespoons of the lemon juice and process again until the dough forms a ball and leaves the side of the bowl. Add extra lemon juice or water if the dough seems dry and crumbly.

Form the dough into a ball, pressing it gently to get rid of cracks, wrap in foil, and chill for 1 hour. Remove from the refrigerator and let the pastry "soften" for 10–15 minutes at room temperature before rolling out.

Put the dough on a lightly floured work surface and roll it out fairly thinly. Use it to line the tart tin, making sure you ease the dough into the corners of the tin without stretching it. Trim off the excess pastry.

To blind bake the tart case, take long, thin strips of foil and fold them over the edge of the tart, to protect and support the sides of the pastry case. Prick the base of the tart all over with a fork. Chill for 30–40 minutes.

Bake the tart case in a preheated oven at 375°F for 8–10 minutes until lightly colored. Beat the egg white with a fork to break it up. Remove the foil strips and brush the inside of the tart case with egg white. Return to the oven for another 8–10 minutes or until the pastry is golden brown and crisp. Let the tart case cool in the tin before unmolding.

index

conversion chart

Weights and measures have been rounded up
or down slightly to make measuring easier.

Volume equivalents:

American	Metric	Imperial
1 teaspoon	5 ml	
1 tablespoon	15 ml	
¼ cup	60 ml	2 fl.oz.
⅓ cup	75 ml	2½ fl.oz.
½ cup	125 ml	4 fl.oz.
⅔ cup	150 ml	5 fl.oz. (¼ pint)
¾ cup	175 ml	6 fl.oz.
1 cup	250 ml	8 fl.oz.

Weight equivalents: **Measurements:**

Imperial	Metric	Inches	Cm
1 oz.	25 g	¼ inch	5 mm
2 oz.	50 g	½ inch	1 cm
3 oz.	75 g	¾ inch	1.5 cm
4 oz.	125 g	1 inch	2.5 cm
5 oz.	150 g	2 inches	5 cm
6 oz.	175 g	3 inches	7 cm
7 oz.	200 g	4 inches	10 cm
8 oz. (½ lb.)	250 g	5 inches	12 cm
9 oz.	275 g	6 inches	15 cm
10 oz.	300 g	7 inches	18 cm
11 oz.	325 g	8 inches	20 cm
12 oz.	375 g	9 inches	23 cm
13 oz.	400 g	10 inches	25 cm
14 oz.	425 g	11 inches	28 cm
15 oz.	475 g	12 inches	30 cm
16 oz. (1 lb.)	500 g		
2 lb.	1 kg		

Oven temperatures:

110°C	(225°F)	Gas ¼
120°C	(250°F)	Gas ½
140°C	(275°F)	Gas 1
150°C	(300°F)	Gas 2
160°C	(325°F)	Gas 3
180°C	(350°F)	Gas 4
190°C	(375°F)	Gas 5
200°C	(400°F)	Gas 6
220°C	(425°F)	Gas 7
230°C	(450°F)	Gas 8
240°C	(475°F)	Gas 9